Wisdom & Vision

The Poetry of Bert Padell

Designed by Victor Zurbel

Published by Aware Publishing Company
P.O. Box 2638, New York, NY 10108

First Edition 1997
Reprint 1998

Designed by Victor Zurbel
Photography processing by Vince Aiosa

Printed in Hong kong

DEDICATION

To my darling family.

My partner - wife and sweetheart - Bobby

My children, the pictures of my life - Ellie, Scott and Wendy.

My second tier of children, thanks for the find of life -
Randi and Gill.

My sweetness of my life, my grandchildren - Dani, Cory,
Jami and Alex.

To my adopted mom and dad - Thank you, (Bobby's
parents), Sylvia and Jerry.

Special thanks to little Duffy Doodles.

To the late Montgomery Clift, my friend for any time around.

To the late Jackie Jensen - Thank you for always being my
teacher and friend.

To the late Mario DeMartini - Thank you for Armand Braiger -
your friend, but best of all our friendship.

My partners in my profession - Thank you for all the years.

To my secretaries, Liz and Wanda - Thanks for always being
there for me.

To all my clients, thank you for the respect, values and love
you share with me.

Thank you to God for the belief given to me that all peoples
should be "color blind".

BERT PADELL
"ACCOUNTANT TO THE STARS"

Bert Padell has got their "numbers".

From his vantage point, across the desk from many of the world's greatest entertainers, performers, sports figures and recording artists, Padell sees beneath the public image to the very humanity of the person, with all of his or her strengths and weaknesses, hopes and fears, and joys and sorrows.

In *Wisdom & Vision,* his fourth volume of poetry, Padell once again shares his deeply felt thoughts and emotions and his uncommon perceptions, that go far beyond the personal, to touch a deep core within all of us.

Born in the Bronx, Padell originally intended to become a baseball player and served as Yankee Bat Boy during the team's glory years. But when injury curtailed his budding baseball career, he pursued law and accounting with equal energy and verve, building a prestigious accounting firm on Broadway. As his lifetime friend Joe DiMaggio has remarked, "In both baseball and business, Bert Padell has exhibited a steady hand, and can still tell the difference between a curve or a sinker whether it comes from the pitching mound or the stock market."

CLIENT LIST

AARON HALL	EXTREME	OKSANA GRISHAK
ALICE COOPER	FATHER MC	ORANGE 9MM
ALICIA KEYS	FITZGERALD SCOTT, SR.	PAT DINIZIO
ANDRE BETTS	FONZI THORTON	PAULINA PORIZKOVA
ANDY PANDA	FOR REAL	PURR
ANGIE FEATHERSTONE	FRANKE PREVITE	R.J. RICE
ANTHONY HAMILTON	FUN LOVING CRIMINALS	RAKIM
ARMA ANDON	GARY KURFIRST	RANDY MYERS
ARNETIA WALKER	GENARD PARKER	REDHEAD KINGPIN
ATLANTA MIX FACTORY	GERALD KELLY	RENEE DIGGS
AUGUST DARNELL	GLORIA GAYNOR	RIC OCASEK
BARRY MICHAEL COOPER	GRACE JONES	RICHARD ADLER
BEN VEREEN	GRAND PUBA	ROBERT DENIRO
BIG DADDY KANE	HARRIS YULIN	ROLANDA WATTS
BRITNEY SPEARS	HARRY BOATSWAIN	RUN DMC
CALVIN RICHARDSON	HECTOR ORTIZ	RUSTY STAUB
CARL BANKS	HURRICANE G	SCOTT LOEBDELL
CARL THOMAS	INTRO	STANLEY TUCCI
CHAD ELLIOTT	IRA SCHICKMAN	STEPHEN BRAY
CHANGING FACES	JOAN JETT	SURYA BONALY
CHRIS HALL	JOHN BERENDT	TALKING HEADS
CHUBB ROCK	JOHN "JELLY BEAN" BENITEZ	TED DEMME
CL SMOOTH	JULIUS LA ROSA	TEDDY PENDERGRASS
CLARK KENT	KEITH SIMS	TERRI ROBINSON
CRAIG MACK	KIMBERLY SCOTT	THE BERMAN BROTHERS
CYNDI LAUPER	KYLE WEST	THE BOGMEN
DARRIN WHITTINGTON	LARRY DVOSKIN	THE BRAXTON SISTERS
DARRYL PEARSON	LEIGH ANN LORD	THE CAULFIELDS
DAVID HALL	LIL SEAN	THE KINKS
DAVID WOLFF	LITTLE INDIAN	THE SMITHEREENS
DEBELAH MORGAN	LORRAINE BRACCO	TIM MOSELEY
DE LA SOUL	LOU PINELLA	TONI BRAXTON
DEVANTE SWING	MARGARET WHITTON	VALARIA MAZA
DONNELL JONES	MARK FIEST	VASSAL BENFORD
DOS FOR SOUL	MARLY MARL	VERONICA
DR. DRE (MTV)	MAURICE STARR	VERUSCHKA VON LEHNDORFF
EARNEST BYNER	METAL CHURCH	VICTOR HAMMER
EDDIE FARRELL	MICHAEL J. MARTINEAU	VINCENT HERBERT
EL GENERAL	MIKHAIL BARYSHNIKOV	WINSTON JOHN
ERIC B	MISSY ELLIOTT	YOUNG LORD
ERNESTO PHILLIPS	MISA	YVETTE MICHELLE
EXCAPE	MONICA PAYNE	YANKEE B
EUGENY PLATOV	MONIE LOVE	
EVERYTHING BUT THE GIRL	MONSTER MAGNET	

INDEX OF POEMS

Wisdom
&Vision

WISDOM AND VISION

Each day I gaze
into space Wondering
what makes life exist
Is it real or just a
wink of an eye?
To others, it is more.

During one's flight of life
many have wisdom
but lack vision.
Passing the same road,
many have vision but
their wisdom has
disappeared.

What God has given
the few — The selected few
It has bestowed
upon them vision of life
And wisdom of life
a true gift.

DIAMONDS IN THE SEA

The sun gazing down touching the sea
looking for wealth.
It appears
Only when the warmth of the sun spreads its rays.
Its touch is Gods movement of the sea.
Specks of diamonds appear
A wealth for all to see
Amazement and wonder
all this freedom.
The diamonds of the sea.

IT'S JUST HER!

I first looked upon her.
She is petite,
Yet taller than the
aged tree within the
forest.
Her height, not in size,
but in stature
Grace she possesses.
Softness in her ways,
her voice pings to the
heart and eyes of your
body
It's just her.

Who is this?
For wanting a kick out
of life,
A feel of wildness, but
in a degree.
She remembers all,
forgets few.

Wants to know when,
where, and why.
It's just her.

Her way of doing for
you
Remembers for the
next time around.
She wants for you and
wants for herself,
giving love and expect-
ing in return.

This woman may sing
for all and breath of
love within the words.
It's just her.
As to her nature a way
of saying
I love, I care and
thank you.

My Kind of Guy

He calls 10:30am sharp, not a second before
He sends candy flowers to my desk or my door
Reminds me of proposals and never breaks his promise
And always gives his Girl her monthly allowance
My birthday, October 7th, he'll never forget
He'll sing in baritone he won't miss a lick
Gently he'll take my hand and lead me through a fiscal land
He helps me make financial plans, and shows me how to take a stand
Forever he fights for what I deserve
And made a vow forever he'll serve
With a watchful eye he won't be shy
And that's why Bertie...

You're My Kind Of Guy

Tom Brnytn

GROWING OLD IS NOT FOR WIMPS

Leaves turn their colors
Flowers bloom and suddenly seasons pass.
Trees of granite are sturdy with the splendor of life
Each grows and is admired because of its years.
The species of man is quite different.
Why???

The Indian worshiped his elders
respected ... learned ... loved ...
had magical thoughts of grandeur of them.
Oriental people always talk of their elders
with value ... with respect ...
and more of love.

Yet we grow old and are afraid of our loved ones.
The respect for them is gone.
The love is there, but fear has invaded our minds.
Eye contact is gone.
The seeking or wanting each other, only if time
permits.
Knowing each other in the now
As years move our lives
Our steps are small ... slower ....
Our clothes of a past style
Our talk more deliberate, and at times not to the
point.
Yet we all ask and want the following
Compassion ... Caring ...
Not pity, but true daring love
The wanting to belong
To have respect for the aging and value what we have
learned can help.
Growing old is not for weaklings because life must
go forward.

DINOSAUR

The moving waters of life
enter my mind and body
and I look back and wonder.
Am I what was, or is there
a new beginning for me?
When as a youth you look and
gaze into the future hoping to be
older and maybe wiser.
Tis true youth is wasted on the young.
Why oh why, I ask?
Must this be our destiny?
During the span of life
we accomplish many deeds of grandeur.
Some are not by choice
Yet, most of us go forward
walking from the dark into a clear sky
Years pass into decades
Looking back in wonderment
Did I do my upmost to be
secure in my life?
Was I just kidding
myself all of the time.
I've accomplished much
But, is it over for me
or just the beginning of a
new episode?

Light shines through
Opening all the time
for those of us who can see
we can learn and
grasp new horizons.

Standing tall with each
Adventure
A dinosaur
to be reckoned with
each minute, hour and
day of our lives.

A File

When first we met
It was strange,
A loudness
Wise remarks
And no gentleness
ever appeared.
Yet, something was there.

His appearance
not striking
but pleasant
A handsome man
He knew he was
that was his problem,
His confidence
Yet One could feel his lack of life
Always thinking someone was
Ready to knock him down

Beat him
Steal from him
Leave him
Laugh at him
Oh! such a pity
For this man of confidence

Friends, he knows not
What they are
They are not the ones that
gave him their hands with wet palms.
Ready at any given time to slip away

The friends that love him
he destroys
Hurts
Just like that of his loved ones
We adore him
Cherish him
And deeply love him
Only to play second to
Unknown knaves
This is a file on a body
A person
who hurts many
And through the years will continue
In the same vein.
Yet, maybe
Someday
The firmament of life will
Awaken him
With a touch
And say
The ones that love him
Caress his eyes
Kiss his eyes
Because they are his light
Which will transcend into
His body, his heart and soul
Only to know, they love him deeply
And hope someday
Life will only
Be filled with love
From him to them
Forever and ever
Till death does part us all
for a movement
Only to awaken in dreams
Wanting love

FAST, QUICK AND GENTLE

The voice was soft yet gruff
Each word came from a thought
Thoughts from many hours of pondering
From words - of experiences of others
Yet, he is fast, quick and gentle.

His life of a strick, rigid process
that created his body.
Each muscle coordinated.
That of a fine tuned watch.
Body and muscle speaking with each command
total obeyance
Yet he is fast, quick and gentle.

Training and more training
thoughts destroying
make it fast, quick
The enemy, his opponent
His thoughts and desires are one

To conqueror, to win, to succeed at all cost
Yet he is fast, quick and gentle

Success was his partner
for almost a decade
The Smell and glory of winning
Then suddenly without warning
carelessly, no training for this event.
He was out
He was not fast, quick and gentle.

Through bad times and bad situations
It captured him
hurt him
betrayed him
At first, left him with no desire
Yet he is fast, quick and gentle.

He has learned
He has prayed
He has desired
From his mistakes
Teaching others of causes because of his woes
A better person
A badge of honor
He wears
A gentle person of wanting
Loving and caring
and he has come alive!

November 2, 1995

Mike Tyson
6740 Tomiyasu
Las Vegas, NV

Hey Bert,

    Forgive me for not writing sooner, I've been running around
with my head cut off. As a matter of fact as I write this letter
to you I'm taking a deposition. Well, I must go now this lawyer
is giving me a hard time. By the way this lawyer is an asshole,
but that's his job. I love you, and stop riding me about my
money, if I go broke, FUCK IT. I just love talking to you as
a man. By the way I'm pretty much set anyway. I am very sorry
that this lawyer is mad because I'm writing this letter to you.

                                    One Love,

                                    Mike Tyson

Burt, I have never been so inspired or felt so empowered by a meeting with someone. Your "success" is a minute part of the world of opportunity that you present to those who are willing to work hard & be guided by you. I have never had a man of your stature reach out his hand to me as you did today. And it is cause for tears for me. Because I think you can see into the hearts of men as I can. And it was just one of those rare moments of human connection. Thanks so much. You are a champion of those who would strive, wish & dream.

Diane Richards
6/24/95

CREATIVE FILM
MANAGEMENT

September 18, 1995

Mr. Bert Padell
156 West 56th St.
New York, NY. 10019

Dear Bert,

When we first met I was too young to appreciate your depth in business and your sensitivity with people.

Now, that I am older and hopefully wiser I would like to add to my appreciation....friendship.

Your friend,

Lou Addesso
President

CREATIVE FILM MANAGEMENT
440 PARK AVENUE SOUTH NEW YORK CITY, N.Y. 10016
PHONE 212.685.6070 FAX 212.545.0976

26

WHAT YOU DO FOR WHAT YOU HAVE!

Each of us should look at ourselves
and ask
If I had, would I change?
My life, my desires
My hopes, my wants
One must always do the following
What you do is to know and be aware
of
Is to do for what you have.
No more no less
This is the essence of life

WHERE WERE YOU AT THIS SWING?

The air was still
No moisture around
Just plain dry
on this day

His arms were tense
with each ounce of strength
Each muscle tolling its weight
The swing started ......
around, around and then around

All were saying
Where were you when Joe Di
did his mighty stentorian swing?

SEASON OF LOVE

All through time we seek the unknown
The season of reason
but this is a disguise
For we really seek love and compassion
for our food of life.
This nurtures our body
Swells our mind
Makes us function
Has us desire
For all seasons of love.

AMEN

The sounds of summer ring aloud
for he is here.
A young dark skinned man
To hear his song.
From the deep core of his soul
knowing his message
will be heard.
Al B.

His voice is that of a bull frog
His verse gentle and sweet.
His melodies are
a sound of love from the heart.
This young man of only two
decades and three
such a handsome smile from
a sturdy muscular frame.
Al B.

He structures the music so it heats to his beat
A miracle of the Gods.
His chant telling all to join in
this man of men
father to his sons
son to Cassandra
husband to Jacqueline
and a friend of mine.
Al B.

Why a friend?
I in need, he is there.
There for me in all phases of life
Oh my friend, a sure meaning and experience of the
word
His word is his bond
A bond we both share when stormy weather occurs in
our paths
God has been good to me
he has gifted me with another son.

A.B.S.OLUTE — PRODUCTIONS
— INCORPORATED —

BERT PADELL

A heart the size of Yankee Stadium,
Clients enuf to fill the seats.

Through an industry of lies,
A challenge he always meets

Tycoon or simply over-broke,
Bert Padell will clear the smoke.

Always your friend and client,

Al B. Sure!

TIME FOR A CHANGE

We had been together by choice
almost fifteen years.
a long time.
You a predominant factor
At times, soft centered with your ideals
while I, always trying to make you strong.
Three sides of the coin
Your opinion, the others and then the truth.

Like falling leaves, time passed
Great accomplishments with
respect, love and always loyalty.
Then suddenly, without warning
Shock, dismay and death to me
Your decisions came across
Not from your spoken
word,
but from another.
Why?
What happened?
What did I do!
The answer, only
It's time for a change!

MADONNA

Happy Birthday
to a very unique person!
thanx for looking out
for me! love Madonna

8/24/95

HOW FRAGILE IS LIFE?

We all resist
and want
The tree sturdy and brazen
Swaying with each gust
Otherwise, life will be over.

We deserve the treasures of life
Some get more, some not a thing
but we must absorb some of its morsels.

The lease we have on life
Expiring at different times for each of us.
Life is what we want, yet fragile.

Oh the sweetness of joy and inspiration --
that
is life.
Each day a treasure
Each day a new beginning
Each day a source of dreams
that make us realize
Positive being and thinking is our only hope
Making life fragile, but durable.

I WANT TO CRY

It happened
Not suddenly
I knew that day would happen.
How would I react?
Would I cry?
Staring into space - I wonder

Did I love her?
or was it just a nothing!
I dearly wanted her love
In return she never gave
anything!

Never gave me herself
oh but why?
My soul
My body
My mind
Asked, why desert me
all I wanted was love.
I want so to cry and cry
Only and only for her!!!
Too no avail - how sorry it is.

BADGE OF COURAGE

I heard them talk
With poise and clarity
Trying to be strong
Trying not to let loose
A crisis
They call it
Never defeated
Never ashamed
He was always a Badge of
Courage
Please dear God, let him be
private
For himself and his family
That is such a small thing
For what he and his co-pilot
have to endure
In life to come
Don't feel sorry for him
he knows and accepts the
challenge of all things.

THE WAY OF LIFE

We strive for success
hoping that it will be our partner
Is this the way of life?
I want to be better than the next person
Or they better than me.
Yet why?
I know I am the same as they are.
The stories of life appear
ever shocking to us all.
Yet we wonder
asking
only a few
Is this the way of life?

CELEBRATING

The day broke through, we are
celebrating
The birth of a new generation
A new life
A new warmth of inspiration
My child's child has arrived
I will celebrate for the rest of
my life.

TWO BECOMES ONE

We have walked in the sand
Our footprints following us through life
With each strive we hold each other tight
Never fearful, because we are one
Oh such a feeling
Belonging
Wanting each other.
Not for a moment but till death do us
part
And then some!!!
Never to think of
or being a part of the word defeat~
We have that energy
only because we are one
Each shall be one's rod and staff
Each shall have one's style
Separate in mind
but one in respect and love
The blueprint of life is ours
tingling and touching us
When we two become one.

I LOVE THEE

Each day
Each hour
Each minute
my thoughts
Desires
Dreams
Are only of you
I love thee
today
tomorrow
and each second
of a distant run
you are my life
my own
Oh I do love thee

BETTER THAN

She is better than
Flies that fly
Flowers that smell
Even thoughts
that have
the colors of rain -
bows.
Dimples that
smooth my
mouth that
make me smile

She is my grandma
I love her today,
tomorrow
and then beyond.

When she puts me on my blanket to crawl
my heart begins to pound
Free at last...free to spread and move in
any direction only because of my grandma

She is my friend
One who I see and then
hours later she leaves
always knowing she will return to see me
and love me.

She is better than
my plug they put in my mouth
she is just better and better and better

Dearest love— Grandma

LITTLE GIRL

What I hope for you
Is only for your eyes
The beauty of the world
as it caresses
each person, from shore to shore
Oh such love, for my little girl.

Beauty beyond a dream
beauty for all to see,
to touch and feel
Just for my little girl.

Peace for your heart
love for your soul
dearness for you alone
Oh, such a person born
into life
I wish you sweetness of love.

TWO FACES

Their profile does astound me
I look and day dream
Dreaming into space
thinking of them
Oh, how beautiful
Their two faces.

It reminds me of them
This picture face
My two loves of life
Their beauty beyond a dream
I will always be their Poppy.

NOT MY MOMENT YET

Time has passed and
I wonder to myself
as I look to the sky.

The wonder of this
gracious world.
It has granted me
The kick of life

The wanting to be
number one
and the down of
being second.
Yet I know that I will fly
and be there when my
time comes.

My dreams will come true
and I know
that the stillness of my life
will erupt and make me
aware and confident
For I know for now. It is not
my moment yet!

NAMES THAT PASS IN TIME

Names that pass in time
Are only names without faces
Yet we remember them
because of their deeds
Yet I will always remember you
with
or without your name
Just you
Just your face for always
I love

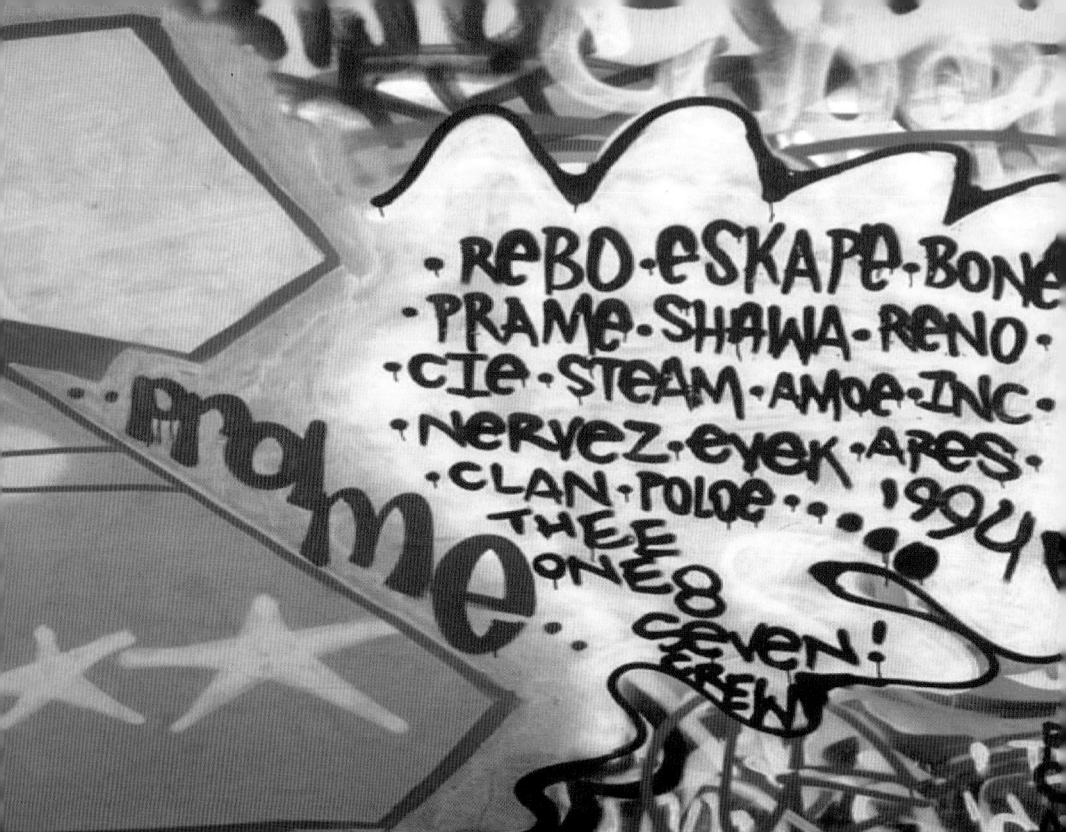

MY KIDS FROM THE STREET

It is lonely
Full of despair
C o l d
Unwanted
Yet my kids from the street are there.

A Need of love
Of Life
Shelter from crime and poverty
Oh, my kids from the street.

They have designed their voice, of rap for expression
A need to voice out.
There will be tomorrow.
But what of yesterday and today.
My kids from the street.

They shall rise out.
They shall desire
They shall conquer
A need to be themselves
A wanting to be needed
Pride in themselves
My kids from the street.

Reality is here
The sense of yes or no shall be theirs
They shall have the wisdom of Solomon.

The kindness and dearness of God
My kids from the street
They will love themselves
And love others.
Love will not be a word to them.
It will be a feeling. A desire. A need
They will have moved from the street to life.

THERE IS GOING TO BE ANOTHER DAY

The day was dark
because "free" was just a word
It shall be reality
Someday ...... Hope shall prevail

On the horizon the air
smells sweet and calm
All is waiting
Hoping!!!

It is arriving
There is going to be another
day for us To be free
As that of the birds that fly
and the air we breathe
for all to rejoice, laughter and love
family, without despair
The day has arrived.

TO BE 'FREE

What is it to say?
I am free.
We take it for granted so many times
Why?
Is being free a privilege,
A desire
A need
A want?
Must one be deserving of freedom
Or does it just come about?

I wonder and ponder
Why is this such a chosen word?
Freedom.

Each of us
All the world
The record of life
we are free and freedom is ours.

Dare someone to take it from us
We respond with vengeance

Take it not for granted.
Cherish it.
Tis the most important task in life
To be free.

SOMETHING NEW

When first we met
It was new for the both of us
through time and trial
We both made mistakes and errors

Learning from each scene of love
Each sense of horror
and each sense of despair
Oh love of my life
We each learned from each other
Grown with each other
I love you desperately
because you are always something new
even though time passes.

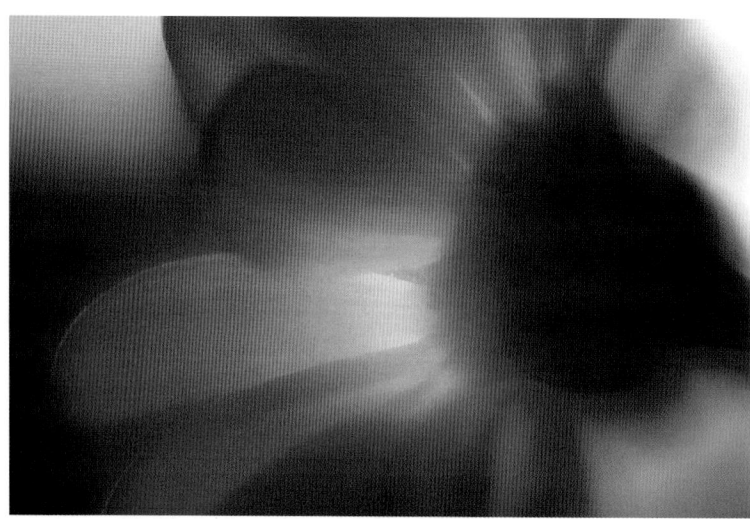

BOX OF CHOCOLATE

Like it said in
the picture show
life is like a box full of
chocolates
Some are tasteful
Some are bitter
Some have nuts for
amusement.
Yet the unknown is
always there
The taste changes
every time
Like a life cycle
This box of chocolates

As we wonder through
the box
each one has its own
secret
and unknowns.
Just like life
we all are ever hoping
for this best of taste.

The taste can only
be its own
and life what we
make of it.
Destroying
Building
Creating us
to one goal.
A risk for the
one that achieves
and the will to
continue to be a man
of his destiny.

THE MEANING OF LOVE

All of us say
I love you
These words with big meaning
Big thought and desire
It is a feeling
of wanting to be part of
something
somebody
the true meaning of love.

MY GRAND CHILD

The day is coming
Like Spring, Winter and Fall
Awakening of time
My thread of life into my heart
My veins, my brain
sparkling my life
No mistakes this time
Time with my grandchild will have
no competition
Life has opened a new awakening
My grandchild is born~!

COLOR BLIND

HE LAUGHS AS I
YET, HE IS DIFFERENT!
HE NOTICED THE TREE SWAYING
WITH EACH GUST
TO MAKE READY FOR SURVIVAL
YET, HE IS DIFFERENT!

HIS BRAIN WANTS WHAT I WANT
HIS SEXUAL NEEDS DESIRE AND CREATE
IMAGINATION TO THE HEART
YET VALUES ARE IN NEED OF CHANGE
TO HIM NO
TO OTHERS MAYBE!
TO THEN OTHERS,THERE MUST BE A CHANGE
YET, HE IS DIFFERENT!

WE TALK THE SAME
CURSE IN THE SAME WAY
OUR EYES GAZE AND NEED MUCH
OF THE WORLD'S TROPHIES
YET, HE IS DIFFERENT!

HE WANTS TO UPGRADE
THE TASTE OF HONEY AND SUGAR
NOT SALT AND BITTER HERBS
THAT IS OF THE PAST
THE FUTURE HE WANTS
NOT TO STAND STILL
YET, HE IS DIFFERENT!

HE WANTS SPARKLING GOLD AND DIAMONDS
BUT JUST FOR SHOW
SECURITY IS HIS REASONS
STATUS FOR HIM IS A NEED
LIKE US ALL
YET, HE IS DIFFERENT!

NOT LIKE BEFORE
HE HAS SPACE IN HIS LIFE FOR
THEM
NOT LIKE HE WAS TREATED
HE DOES LOVE
AND WANTS IT IN RETURN
YET, HE IS DIFFERENT!
HIS CHILDREN HAVE BECOME
NEEDED

LOVE HE SO DESIRES,
NEEDS, AND CHERISHES
TO KNOW THAT THIS IS REAL
TO HIM.
IS GOD'S GIFT TO HIM
YET, HE IS DIFFERENT!
DIFFERENT HE IS NOT!
DIFFERENT SINCE YOU ARE
COLOR BLIND MY FRIEND
IN THIS RESPECT ONLY
THE WIND WILL BLOW
THE SPRING WILL BRING LIFE
ANEW
THE SUMMER WILL
STAND STILL
AND WAIT AWHILE FOR THE
LEAVES TO LIFE
HE IS LIKE US ALL.

MY EYES MIGHT BE
COLORED BLIND!
YET, I WANT FOR HIM
TO WALK WITH MEN OF MEN
AND NEVER LOOSE THE
TOUCH
AND FEELINGS OF THEM.
WE ALL ARE
ONE TO ANOTHER
EQUAL IN EACH WAY
GOD'S CHILDREN.

THE WILL OF GOD

**Whatever there is
Whatever there is said
Whatever it feels or
Whatever it might be
This only occurs from
the will of God.**

THE MEETING OF STRANGERS

I never looked at your eyes.

Your face questions me.

Is your hair brown?

The voice you speak enchants me;

The time will come when we shall

meet.

LIVING EACH DAY

Each day of your life
Reminds oneself of the touch of rain
The warmth of the sun against one's body.
The sky, the firmament of God
Its silky whiteness
Guarding the bluest color of life
Brightness of the day
Darkness of night!
Spears in the night
Riding and descending into life
This is for all to see
assuming and accepting
each day as a lifetime
Today is the beginning of
the first day of your life.
Living each day as if it were the last.
We know not what is to come,
except the day present...
The beginning of a lifetime.

ANY ROAD WE TRAVEL

I will be there for you
Through the darkest cloud
The muddiest road
Any road we go on,
will bring us together
Your needs will be mine
Love for you without a
twinkle of a thought
My friend, for any road you travel
I will be there for you.

THEY PLAY MUSIC

You first meet them.
They are young
The music makes their name
Beautiful through its softness
This beauty is black.

They come from a place
Unknown to the mass.
Yet, it is their place
home and comfort for them.
The best that they can do is have music
conquer us all.

Each one of them has God's gift
Two sets of brothers and
their golden voices.
Voices that make your heart beat faster
For the finesse, sweetness and softness.

The other set
create the sound
create the verse
create the mood
The feelings of love and desire

Expression beyond the next time around
The brothers four.

They were just put together
by a silent man
a stern but precise individual
a creator of character
this their fifth silent member.

God
They are members of your vision
Your call
Your love
and desires
They play music for us all
The footprints of this sound will
always be imprinted.

WHAT UP MY FAVORITE NIG....
OOOPS - SORRY - ANYWAY....BESIDES
MY FATHER, YOU ARE THE ONLY OTHER
MAN I LOOK UP 2 & RESPECT, And
WILL ALWAYS CHERISH THE THINGS
YOU'VE TAUGHT ME, GOD PUTS PEOPLE
IN OUR LIVES FOR A REASON SO I
THANK HIM EVERY DAY FOR YOU - YOU'RE
A BLESSING...WELL I COULD GO ON
BUT WE'LL HAVE MANY ~~~~~ MORE
~~DAYS~~ TOGETHER 2 APPRECIATE EACH OTHER
YEARS

THANK YOU 4 ALL
DA' STRESS
w/LOVE DEVANTE

I HAVE 3 people 2 THANK 4 my EXISTANCE 1. GOD - FOR MAKING ME, HAVING MERCY ON ME, AND WATCHING OUT 4 ME, And BLESSING ME WITH TALENT + BEING A FRIEND)
2. MY FATHER AND MOTHER - FOR RAISING ME, BELIEVING IN ME, LOVING ME, TEACHING ME BEING THERE 4 ME
3. BERT PADELL - FOR TAKING CARE OF ME, TRUSTING ME, BEING A FRIEND, LOOKING AFTER ME BEING THERE

May U LIVE 4ever
Bert

One thing's for sure ~
They don't make 'em like you anymore!
Thanks 4 everything

HAPPY BIRTHDAY

*1 GUY

GIVE THANKS

For all we have
Small or large
For those who have noth-
ing
Please give to them
a little of the plenty
For they know and will be
thankful of the little
thanks, just for that!

AN INSULT TO GOD

Please believe
To Hate
To Dishonor
Is an insult to God.
His color
His religion.
Her being is for all to
believe in.
Often God will say
This is my personal
insult.

IMPORTANCE

It is a word
A meaning to many
less to some
Yet when one thinks
Another doesn't
Why! - Oh, Why!
If all could think
And, think of the next guy
When not answering or replying

We would all feel,
act and love differently.
So please dear person
My importance, is much to me
Consider me.

With the turn of life
Your answer to me
Makes my day.

GIVE US OUR VALUES

We lost them
I hope not forever
They were so precious to us
They belonged to us all
Yet, we gave them away
This is what we had whether rich or poor
We could only give them away
no one could take from us
Our values of life.

AFRAID OF COLOR

I look into the mirror
and wonder
Why are they afraid?
I laugh like they do
Cry from despair
Love with passion
Desire for love
Live with poverty
Strive for richness
Why are they so afraid?

They are big in size, like me
and small too!!
Curse and swear, at times, for no reason, like me
Yet is there reason - why afraid?
Oh God - why - ?

I do believe the truthfulness of it all
to be afraid of my color
that God gave me
Accept me for what I am
Judge me for myself, not my skin
My color is beautiful and pure
and so is yours.
I do love all
Love me for myself
We are all color blind in God's eyes.

TO LIKE EVERYBODY

Tis the season
To be fair
gentle and loving

We all ask why, should we?
because it is the time!
The place for to look at thy neighbor
and say, love thy fellow man.

If we could have
the same feeling
all year round
it would be a better place
to be
to live
and love by.

When we ask God
Remember, he helps those who
helps oneself
Not to be selfish
Yet each of us have
love and charity within
The most important thought we all have
Is to love and like each other!!

A PLACE TO BE

The feeling
The joy
the hapiness
of only
to know
I have a place to be

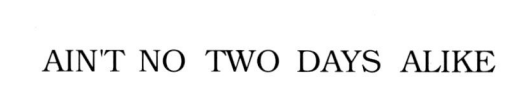

AIN'T NO TWO DAYS ALIKE

This day the sun came
and peeked at me
I wonder
Is this the same for tomorrow?
No !!!
Ain't no two days alike.

THORNS OF LIFE

I look at the beauty
of God's creations
gentle, soft
Colors of beauty in all shades
Protecting its flower
by the thorns at its stem
This the thorns of Life.

Life itself.
Living for today
not yesterday
Or the day to come.
Each day an episode
An experience
A happening
A beginning
of a new horizon
Within the thorns of life.

We meet all kinds of people in life.
Some never call
When we are anxiously awaiting an answer
Some talk of reason
and positive ideas
Yet, only think of negativity
and hurt.
Words of destruction and not the desire
to begin a new beginning.
This the thorns of life

One, must be astute
Kind and gentle to know
there will be change
when the thorns of life
seem to conquer all.

The new coming
The new start
The chance, that things will change
That the thorns will disappear
The protection unnecessary
The rose clean and
beautiful with color.
The aroma caressing one's senses
The thorns of life gone
For today, tomorrow and the next
time around.

WHO CARES WHO WON

At last we met
My father and I
To play the game
I waited for

All my life
Waiting!
To beat him

It started
minute by minute
we played

Oh yes, he is with me
Only me -
Playing this game with me
He and he only loves me

The game is over
over and over
They ask who won
Who cares who won.

AND YOU TO ME

I look into your face
and can see within myself
You have helped me
Conquer much.

I can see when it is the darkest
I can laugh when there appears to be joy.
Whatever shall be, I shall stand strong
enduring the foul talk.

My love for you
Is that of my love for myself
For one can not love another
Unless one loves thyself.

I do love thee
for all times
good or bad
content or not so
today, tomorrow and next time
You are my wish
And you to me
Till death does part us.

EACH OTHER

We first met
Our eyes touched
The senses of life
we both endured
the innocence of our friendship
Did explode
We are the most to each other.
Fame and dollars
are not our life
may it never change
The soul of the seasons
we march to
We are there for each other
Everytime around.

I WAS LOST FOR AWHILE

It happened when I looked back
To all the fondest dreams
Thoughts
Ideals
Loves
Knowing I was not lost
Finding myself, because of you.

LOVING YOU

To watch the water tingling down
with each drop and morsel of
life's wanting is my exacting
love and desire for you
each day breaking with seasons of time
our love enduring and aging with time
Loving you
is wanting you
today
tomorrow
and next time around
the new horizon has begun
with each meeting, each talk
each kiss.
This is loving you.

TO BE TOUCHED

To be wanted
Needed by one or the mass
Is the fundamental need for us.
Yet the most important promise to oneself
Is the need to be touched.
Touched for the sign and hope of love
Its feeling is everything; the best of life
It makes the mind swell with a hungry appetite.

To be touched
Is the wonder strive of life
Tis the firmament of being
Each sign of existence is the human touch.

SEE YOU IN FIVE

Here is a friend
I met in time a decade less four.
If I ever needed him
He is there.
Good times or bad
It works together.
I would do for him
like he would do for me.
And I shall see him in five!

Dear
Bert, Happy Happy Birthday!
Happy, love,
Bob

p.s "See you in five!"

Aug 24, 1995

ROBERT DE NIRO

A GREAT TRUTH

The clothes of a slave
is not the judgement of what he is.
The thoughts of man
must be free and clear.
The color of a man's skin
is not the judge of what he is
or who he is.
Justice is better than injustice.
One love for us
as to one truth
that all men are equal.
This is and will always be the great
truth of life.

DARKNESS

The darkness of life is what I
remembered
Not red or the touch of yellow.
But the light, will it shine in?
To open my eyes
and witness life
not despair.
All are not bad without feelings,
or loyalty
or Integrity.
Oh, why do we need?
We all need light,
not darkness from each other.

A FRIEND PASSING AWAY

The day has passed
A friend is lost
Yet, he is not
he will always be remembered
Loved and
Cherished
You will meet him in the beyond.

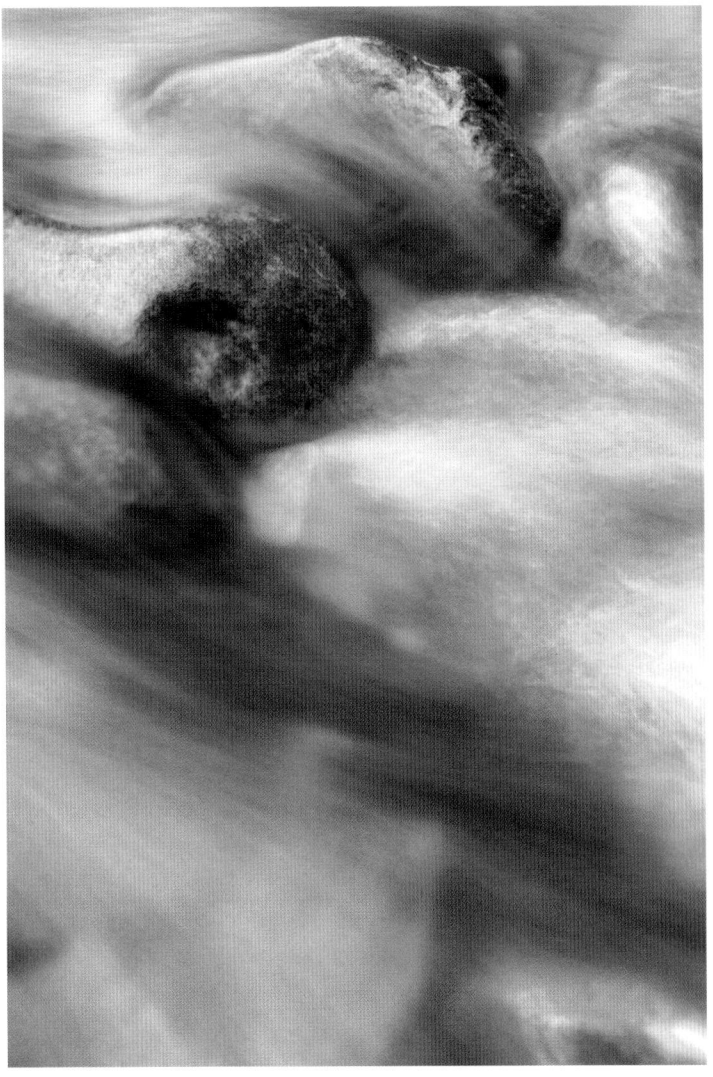

CHILDHOOD OF OUR NATION

In life, we experience many happenings.
In the beginning of our nation, we all came aboard
To seek adventure
To find a new nation.
We were children in a new beginning.
Unfortunately, others were there first.
They were free and carefree
Believed in nature, cared for beings.
Then suddenly without warning
We appeared.
We destroyed.
Took without title.
Invaded their being
Hostile to all of their belongings.
Made treaties of agreements,
Only to break the broken arrow of
despair and disappointment.
Their status was that of the dead Buffalo
in the trails.
This useless happening
for what, for why --
How does one treat a child or Father of
a nation --
We did
We wanted
We conquered
Without warning of want
This nation of all people
Divided and conquered the Red Man
for lack of reason.
This was the beginning of the childhood
of our nation.

IS MONEY WORTH THE LIE

He was a man of what I thought
was integrity— yet I was wrong

I see he is doubtful, lying for money
Compromising himself
His soul
His thoughts

Is money worth it
Why?

GOD DOES NOT PROMISE TOMORROW

There are prayers
There are thoughts
There are desires
There are wantings
Each of us should live for today
All its glories
All its joys and at times
its nasty happenings
For all we can be assured
God does not promise us tomorrow
So live for the time of today.

TO CARE FOR US

To believe that we are all good
To believe that God is with us at all times
To believe in one's self.
To believe in love of life
That my fellow man is the same.
No matter the call of one's beliefs,
Yet most of all not what one looks like
The way he feels
We should be colored blind in every day life
And love thy goodness
True love and sincere feelings for each
other
God has looked on us all
And believes in us, cares for us all
Loves us in perpetuity.

TO BE REAL

To be what God asked you to be
To be Real,
To yourself
To your mind
Your body, your being
Never afraid of a shadow
Shadows don't exist
Foul weather never seen.
Real is what we all try to achieve
Some never make it
While few succeed
They are the few
and beautiful
Real to them
Real inside
And, Real to life.

A TIME TO LIVE - A TIME TO DIE

This is our time to live
To live each second of a distant run
To catch each minute and never let it go
For life is the kingdom
To enjoy
To love
To be happy
It will last
How long?
Nobody knows!
Except within us
To feel the time has come
This time has arived
For it is the time to die.

WHITE RAIN

The clouds crowed together
Their whiteness slowly disappeared
Each asking what is happening?
Then the rain came.

It started with a light cold wet rain.
Then slowly the warmest of the air spread over.
The warmness conquered the air, the moisture was
heavy,
the rain continued
It began as if it was a war
The rain screeched on and on crying
The whiteness touched the ground.
The skies were sad and very tired
Whiteness had appeared from the rain
to tell us of a new beginning of freshness.

THE DOVE SHALL FLY

Suddenly without warning
A cry
A shot
Horror
the fallen Dove
The olive branch his idea
even during times of despair
He fought for his ideals
and his thoughts were always of peace for all.
Disaster happened
We shall not forget this warrior's statement
He shall fly enabling us to see
the Dove of peace and security.

WE ARE NOT THE SAME

Why is this happening?
You hate me
for no reason
except one
I am black, you white
This will always be.

I cry
I laugh
I smile
I need what you need
and I am black, you white

You have never been to my home
Or me to yours
My children don't play with your children
Only, because I am black and you are white.

As much as you care for me
the others don't
They pretend.
We are not the same
God didn't intend this
Yet people have willed it

Will it change?
Only if you feel the way I do.
Accept what I have never had.
Believe it has been hard
from decade to decade.

In a room with two equals
One black, one white
there is a difference before we speak.

Oh my friend, I am black
I am proud strong and different
Different because all have made it that way

For a beginning you my white friend
can we start now?
I do sincerely
care and
love you,
Can we be the ones to prove
we are the same?

THE BEST I CAN

There are many things one sees
and hears in lifetime.
Good or evil being done to each other.
There are a few that keep doing the good
Yet nothing happens.

The effort is there
Sensitivity is all around
nothing seems to happen.
Soul searching from within
Tireless motion
Stress
Sleepless nights
Trying to do one's best.
Then the day came when the best came.
Closed, done, finished.
Love,
It has ended
The best has happened.

TRAITORS DAY & NIGHT

The day began
And then came to rest
Three men in my life
In my heart, in my trust
Allowing my body and soul
to beckon with delight
Only to be destroyed
The disappointment of their manner and behavior
They became the evils
In the foxhole I would never sleep
Frightened because of their devious character
The lowest of men
Men that my God could never accept
Greed, money and gossip their food for life
Now traitors, throughout the long days & nights.

BARRY WINE

November 20, 1996

BERT,

CONGRATULATIONS ON YOUR TOFU CHEESECAKE. I THINK IT
IS TERRIFIC.

I TRIED IT LAST NIGHT RIGHT OUT OF THE REFRIGERATOR AND
AGAIN FOR LUNCH AT ROOM TEMPERATURE.

I'M GOING TO TRY A COUPLE OF EXPERIMENTS. IS THIS
EXACTLY THE RECIPE IN WENDY DIAMOND'S BOOK? I WANT
TO SEE IF IT WILL FREEZE AND I ALSO WANT TO DO ONE WITH
ONLY VANILLA AND LEMON AND SEE IF PEOPLE CAN TELL IT
APART FROM WHAT THEY CALL "PLAIN NEW YORK
CHEESECAKE".

I'M GOING TO CALIFORNIA NEXT WEEK BUT WILL RETURN
YOUR SPRING FORM BEFORE I GO . IF I DON'T GET TO THE
EXPERIMENTS THIS WEEK, I'LL DO THEM AS SOON AS I RETURN.
IF YOU CAN GIVE ME ANY SPECIAL HINTS, EITHER CALL OR
FAX ME WITH INSTRUCTIONS.

HOPE THAT SOMETHING CAN COME OF THIS. I ALWAYS KNEW
THAT LAWYERS MADE GREAT COOKS BUT NOW I CAN SAY THE
SAME THING ABOUT AT LEAST ONE ACCOUNTANT.

BEST

THE DREAM TEAM

We all met to accomplish our goal
To make a happening
This sturdy team of five
To challenge all odds
Be able to make the storm disappear
And make a rainbow appear
This was for Toni
With all minds together
Ready for battle
Words and more words— change after change
This Dream Team never waiving or despairing
for lack of results
It is done these men of reason and stature
Toni's own Dream Team

Breath of Fresh Air
by Damian Shelbe

Stifled, out of breath, with no, where to turn
Although we did things not many other artists would do
Without internal ties our music still was unheard
Knowone called it average, nor weak, nor lacking flavor
So how was it knowone would help us out?
That's when God granted us favor
We met a man with no reason at all to help
out persons he'd never met
When others of lower stature gave nothing
but disregard and neglect
At first I must admit I couldn't figure
what was intended, or is he being facetious
But now I've calmed down, and I go with
the flow & figure its for the purest of reasons
No hot air when words you utter discourage
a being so hungry and persistent
To escape the jaws of life itself and become
just another statistic
For even if nothin comes of this, the concern and
help you gave sparked a new flame, a second wind
And now I know I do have what it takes to
Satisfy my outer world, as well as within
May what started out as coincidental, last and endure
When the time comes for guidance for real I know
that I have backing for sure
Words cannot express the thanks and gratitude
I feel for the helping hand you've lent
Perhaps maybe we can go beyond acquaintances,
and business, and be friends

(To Bert Padell for showing concern
to someone who knowone is concerned with.)

98

CELEBRATING HER LIFE

Never knew her
Yet we all did
She became one of us
Never estranged from the mass
Her smile of warmth and desire
A desire to help
A love unconditional to us all
She is and will always be our Princess
A genuine Queen of hearts, mind and soul
The flag will always remain at half mast
in memory and love.

Rusty Staub

May 20, 1996

Obviously, Bert Padell is a top professional business manager. You always know where you stand with Bert, he doesn't sugar-coat it. But, Bert, to me is one of the really caring people I have met in my life.

Whenever you are most in need, he seems to be around giving you good, solid advice and he gives you that advice in a way that makes you understand he has your best interest in heart.

I'm pleased to call him my friend.

Rusty Staub

RUSTY

His name is known
Far and Wide
Baseball his fame
Restaurants his second love
The taste of good wine
and need of a good rib
His name spread worldwide
Rusty

Roar of the crowd
Hit the ball over the fence
Called many times
cold and stiff
right from the bench
Without a warm up
His swing and strike of the bat
for Rusty had come through
As usual a hit to an empty space
This was Rusty

A soft voice
we all heard over the air
To tell us how the team played
It stirred us to a high pressure degree

This man, a creative version
Oh such a man
He gave us his imagination
He gave us his insight
his warmth of life
His talk of real life
this stentorian man
Rusty

To write of this man
is a pleasure in itself
There are few and far between
That have so much to offer
He is so much and takes so little
He walks and talks
with Kings
for all of us
this man, Rusty

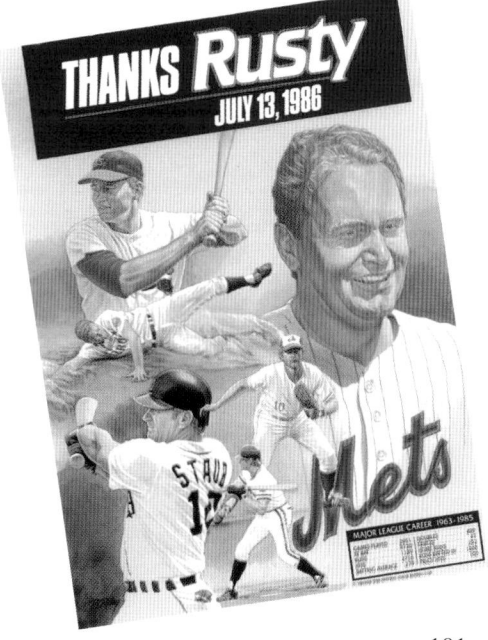

How I Became a Batboy for the New York Yankees

BY BERT PADELL

$\mathbf{M}$y story of becoming the batboy for the New York Yankees in 1949 and 1950 is one for the records.

In January, 1948, at the young age of 14, I sent letters to the New York Giants, New York Yankees, and the Brooklyn Dodgers, inquiring how to become their batboy. I received replies from each team informing me that all the batboy jobs were taken. Not admitting defeat or taking no for an answer, I went directly to the Yankee ticket office, then located on 58th Street and Fifth Avenue, to inquire in person about getting the job. I asked to see George Weiss who was general manager of the Yankees. When I was informed that he was not there, 1 walked to the New York Giants ticket office at 42nd Street and Sixth Avenue to try them. It was pouring rain and I didn't have a raincoat or umbrella. When I arrived, in addition to be soaking wet from the rain, this 14 year old aspiring batboy had to desperately use the bathroom facilities. I vividly recall to this day squeezing my legs together trying to hold it in.

Behind the cage at the ticket counter were the Giant personnel, including Barney O'Toole, the head usher and ticket manager for the Polo Grounds. (I later became a very good friend of Barney's, but at the time he only knew me as the kid he had to chase because I was always hustling around trying to get the players' autographs.) When I told Barney that I wanted to see Horace Stoneham, the president of the New York Giants, he said "Look. kid, you can't see Horace because he isn't here." Just then, I spotted Horace going to the fountain for a drink. I said "1'm not leaving until I see Horace Stoneham, and there he is!" In the meantime, a noticeably large puddle had circled beneath me because I was soaking wet. Barney pointed to the puddle and said, "Look kid, just go to the bathroom because you are making a big mess." I went to the bathroom and came back with towels and wiped up all the puddles of water. Then I stood there and refused to move. I insisted, "I'm not leaving until I see Horace Stoneham." After an hour had passed, he said, "Hey, kid, do me a favor...take this guy's number, and annoy *him.* His name is Eddie Logan, the clubhouse manager for the New York Giants, and he lives on West 170th Street "

I ran right out to catch the next subway train to 170th Street. As I walked into the lobby of his building I noticed a man with glasses leaving with a lady. For some reason, we both stared at each other. When I rang the doorbell of Eddie Logan's apartment, the babysitter informed me that he just left for the movies, and I realized that the man I had just been staring at, was him.

The babysitter told me to come back the next day at 10 A.M. I thought she said *7 A.M.* and to be on the safe side, as well as impress him, I arrived at 6 A.M. When I rang the bell at that ungodly hour, Mr. Logan came to the door groggy, without his glasses on. *Who the hell are you?", he cursed. "Don't you know what time it is?" I replied," I am Bert Padell. I was here to see you yesterday and your babysitter told me to come back today." He said "Yeah~ but you were told to come at 10 A.M. not 6 A.M!" I said, "I'm sorry, I thought she said 7 A.M. and I got here early to impress you."

He asked me what I wanted, after putting on his glasses and rubbing his eyes, as he could hardly see this early in the morning. I said, "Look, I'm sorry, but I wanted to see you about being the Giant's batboy." He told me they already had a batboy named Bobby Sealing, and had also hired a visiting batboy, but wasn't sure if he was going to keep the job because he was studying to be a priest, and his mother did not want him to be in the close proximity of people who were cursing, smoking, drinking and chasing women. Therefore, he would have to let me know next Saturday. But at 10 A.M. not 6:00 A.M!

I arrived at 10:00 A.M. the following Saturday, and asked, 'Does the visiting batboy still have the job?" He said, "I'm sorry Bert, he does." I said, "Please, I will do anything. Make me the *assistant* visiting batboy. I will help both sides. I will do anything. I will even pick up spit." "What did you say," he asked. I said, "I will pick up spit. Please give me a chance". I just wouldn't let up and take no for an answer. Then he asked me what my religion was. When I told him that I was Jewish, he shouted at me, "No wonder you're so pushy... you're a dirty son of a bitch Jew!" But I didn't let it bother me, I kept on talking to him. He asked me, "Didn't you hear what I said?" I replied, "Eddie , I'm just a little kid, and all I want is the job. I'm a good ball player and good worker. Please give me a job as the assistant visiting batboy. Please."

He looked at me and said, "You know kid, I really like you a lot. One, because you said that you will pick up spit and do anything to get the job, and two, when I insulted your religion, you just disregarded it because you know that is what you have to do when you are a little guy here. People often say things they do not really mean, but you have to be able to take it and realize that you are a low man on the totem pole." I said, "Sir, I know that. All I want is a job." He said, 'Tell you what, you got the job as *assistant visiting batboy*. I'm making this new position available just for you. And not only that, I'll pay you two dollars a day." "You're going to pay me!", I responded. "Geez, I didn't expect to get paid!" I left his house with tears in my eyes. I just couldn't believe that this young kid from the Bronx could become assistant visiting batboy of the New York Giants!

On my first day of work. I met Bobo Newsom, Jack Lohrke, and Whitey Lockman, and introduced myself: "Hi. I'm Bert Padell..the assistant visiting batboy." They said, "Boy, you have a long title." I agreed, "Yeah, but I love it." They became my pals, and I started to catch batting practice with them in civilian street clothes. At the time Mel Ott was the manager, and when they fired him, Leo Durocher became the Manager. When he saw me catching batting practice in civilian clothes he told the team to give me a Giants uniform and they did.

I would throw the ball around the in-field when they had the first and second string catchers and then they gave me a chance to throw it around to all the ball players. I had a good arm, and could really throw the ball. Then one day, the visiting batboy unfortunately got killed in a hunting accident, and I took over his position. The visiting clubhouse manager "Little Pete" Previte also worked at Yankee stadium, and in August, when the Yankee batboy had to go on a two-week training duty, who did he ask to be the Yankee batboy'? Me! I went over to Yankee Stadium for two weeks. On my first day there, Bill Bevens, the Yankee pitcher, was looking for a catcher, and bingo, I said, "Here I am. I can catch." He pitched to me with all of his might and strength, and I threw it back faster than him. He was so proud of me. Meanwhile, I had a little glove and my hands were swollen from catching his fast balls. When I entered the clubhouse, everybody was around Bill's locker talking about me, "Boy this kid catches better than Yogi." Cliff Mapes spotted me and starred at my glove. He said, "Geez, kid, let me see your glove." He put on my glove and pounced fist into it, hurting his hand. (And one of Cliff Mapes' hands was the size of both of my hands. He grabbed my hand, and looked at the bruise where I was catching. He shouted, "Kid you can't catch with this glove! You have to wear a sponge. Does anybody have a catchers' glove for him?" Charlie Silvera said, "I have an extra one." and gave me his catchers glove. From then on, everyday another pitcher came to me to catch for them. Frank "Spec" Shea, Allie Reynolds, Vic Rashi and Ed Lopat had me all catch for them. It was just tremendous!

After the season ended, the Yankees told me that they would like me to be their batboy for the 1949 season. I said, "I can't unless I speak to Eddie Logan, the clubhouse manager for the Giants, because he gave me my first chance." 1 went over to Eddie Logan, and said, 'Eddie, would it be alright if I went to the Yankees to be their batboy for the 1949 season?" He said, "Bert, there's not a kid 1 know that would even ask for permission, and you did because you are an exceptionally special kid. Sure you can go. Good luck." When I went over, a headline in the New York Sun appeared: "Giants Trade Batboy to New York Yankees." They were writing about me! And so in the spring of 1949, I became the Yankee batboy. I would catch for different pitchers. I even helped Joe DiMaggio when he had a heel problem. I would train with him, play outfield, shortstop, pitch to him and do anything and everything to enable him to get in shape. 1 always did the very best 1 could for all the New York Yankees.

1 can recall an episode as Yankee batboy that should be in all the books and records. In the summer of 1949, we were two games behind and had three games left in the season. We were playing the Boston Red Sox at home on Friday night, Saturday, and Sunday. We had to win all three games in order to win the pennant. If we lost any of the games, the season would be over for us. The game was proceeding on Friday nights and in one of the late innings, Joe McCarthy, manager of the Boston Red Sox, ran out of the dugout screaming and yelling at the umpire. The umpire called time out and listened to Joe and started to laugh. He called Casey Stengel, manager of the New York Yankees, to come out and talk with him. Casey Stengel came out of the

dugout, and walked over to the umpire and listened tentatively. He took off his hat and scratched his head and started to laugh. He then walked over to me as I was kneeling next to the batter on the deck and told me, "The umpire said you were stealing signals and have to be confined to the dugout for the remainder of the game. Conratulations, kid. You have just made the history books as the first batboy to be kicked out of a game for stealing signals." But he also told me not to take it too seriously.

When I arrived at the dugout, I was greeted by Vic Raschi, one of the ace Yankee pitchers. He laughed and said, "You made the history books, kid." During the remainder of the game, I ran to and from the dugout to tender the bats for the club. This was a great experience in the summer of 1949 that I will relive over and over again.